W9-BAF-430

CHILDREN 595.7 ALLEN
Allen, Judy
Are you a grasshopper?

Central

APR 0 1 2003

CENTRAL LIBRARY

Backyard Books

Are you a Grasshopper?

KINGFISHER
Larousse Kingfisher Chambers Inc.
80 Maiden Lane
New York, New York 10038
www.kingfisherpub.com

First published in 2002

1 3 5 7 9 10 8 6 4 2

1TR/1201/TWP/GRS/150NYM

Copyright © Kingfisher Publications Plc 2002
Text copyright © Judy Allen 2002

All rights reserved under International
and Pan-American Copyright Conventions

LIBRARY OF CONGRESS CATALOGING-IN-PUBLICATION DATA

Allen, Judy.

Are you a grasshopper? / by Judy Allen; illustrated by Tudor Humphries.—1st ed.

p. cm.—(Backyard books)

ISBN 0-7534-5366-5

1. Grasshoppers—Juvenile Literature. [1. Grasshoppers.] I. Humphries, Tudor, ill. II. Title.

QL508.A2 A64 2001

595.7'26—dc21

Editor: Carron Brown
Series Designer: Jane Buckley

Printed in Singapore

Backyard Books

Are You a Grasshopper?

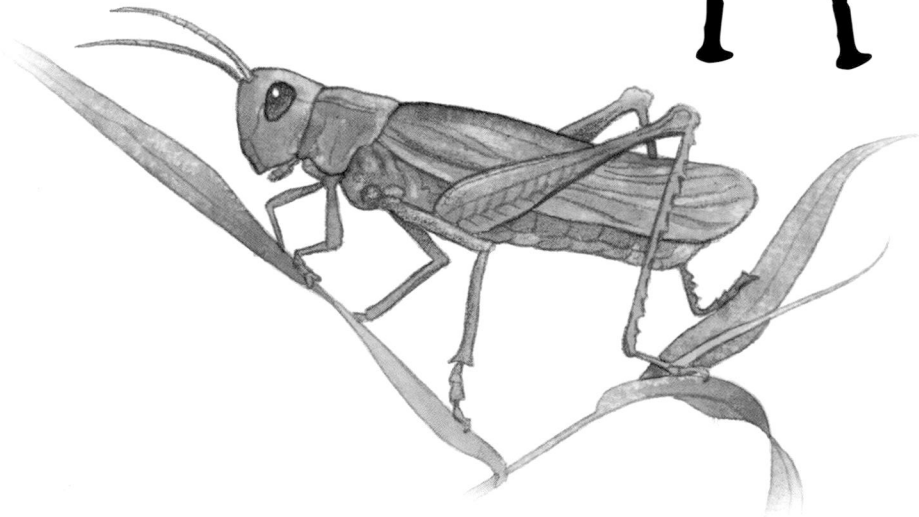

Judy Allen and Tudor Humphries

KINGfISHER
NEW YORK

Are you a grasshopper?

If you are, your mother looks like this.

Your father looks much the same.

Your mother laid her eggs
at the end of the summer.
She laid them deep in the grass,
just under the ground,
and covered them in frothy stuff.
The froth hardened into a pod
to keep the eggs safe.

You and your brothers
and sisters slept in
your eggs all winter—
but now it's spring.

Time to hatch.

Push all together
to get out of the pod.

You look a little like
a tiny worm, but
that's only because
you're wrapped in a
worm-shaped covering.

So unwrap yourself.

You're still tiny, and you don't have
any wings, but now you look
like a grasshopper.

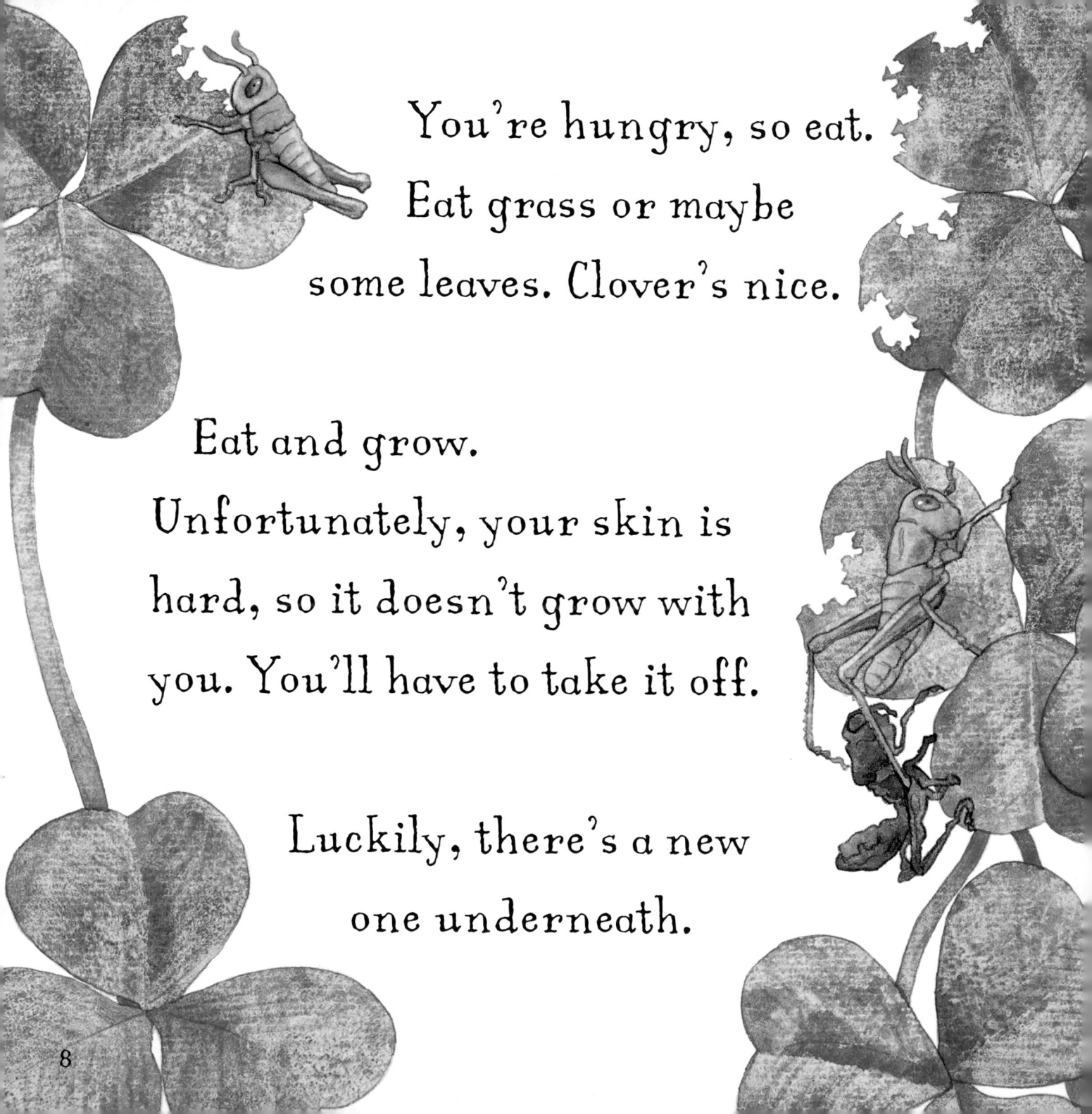

You're hungry, so eat.
Eat grass or maybe
some leaves. Clover's nice.

Eat and grow.
Unfortunately, your skin is
hard, so it doesn't grow with
you. You'll have to take it off.

Luckily, there's a new
one underneath.

Eat and grow and change your skin again. Now you have wing buds on your back.

Change your skin again.

Now you have small, stubby wings.

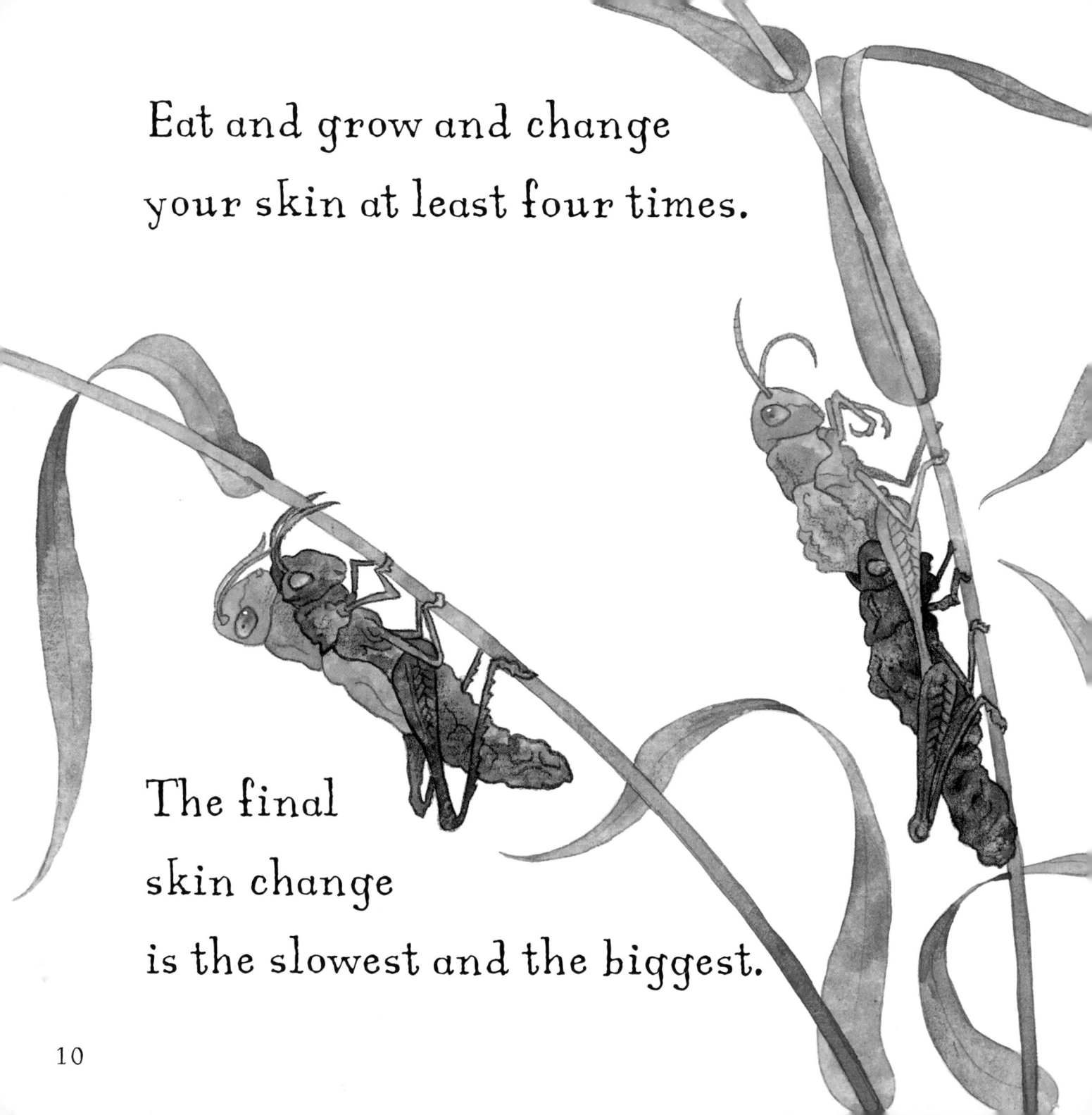

Eat and grow and change
your skin at least four times.

The final
skin change
is the slowest and the biggest.

Struggle out of your old
skin and hang from
a grass stem

while your wings
grow to full size.

At last
you are a fully grown grasshopper.

You're bigger and stronger than before.
You have six legs, two pairs of wings,
two large eyes, and two short feelers.

You have tiny ear holes on the sides
of your body, above your
back pair of legs.

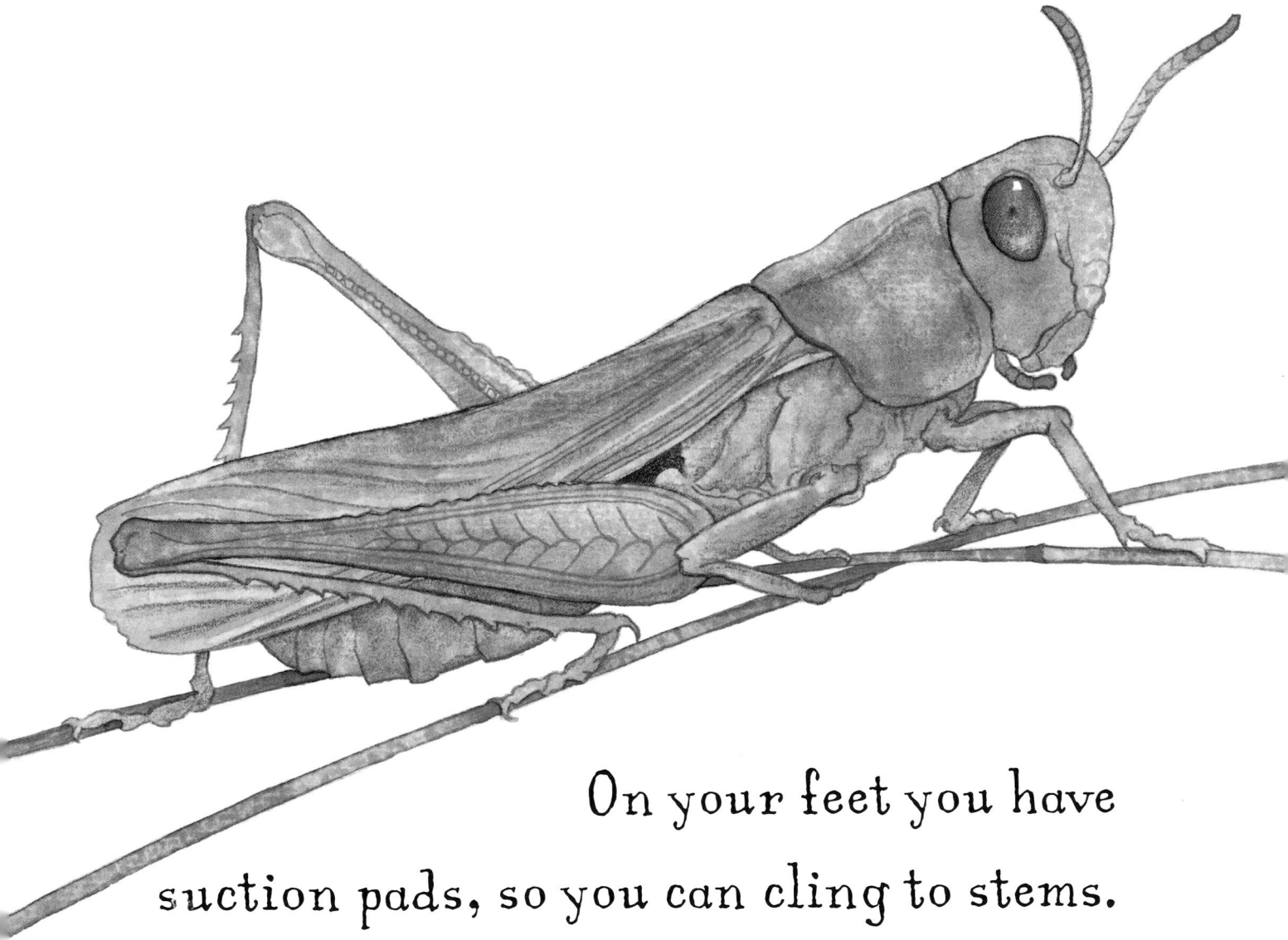

On your feet you have suction pads, so you can cling to stems. Beside your mouth you have palpi, like tiny fingers, to help push in your food.

This is a bush cricket.

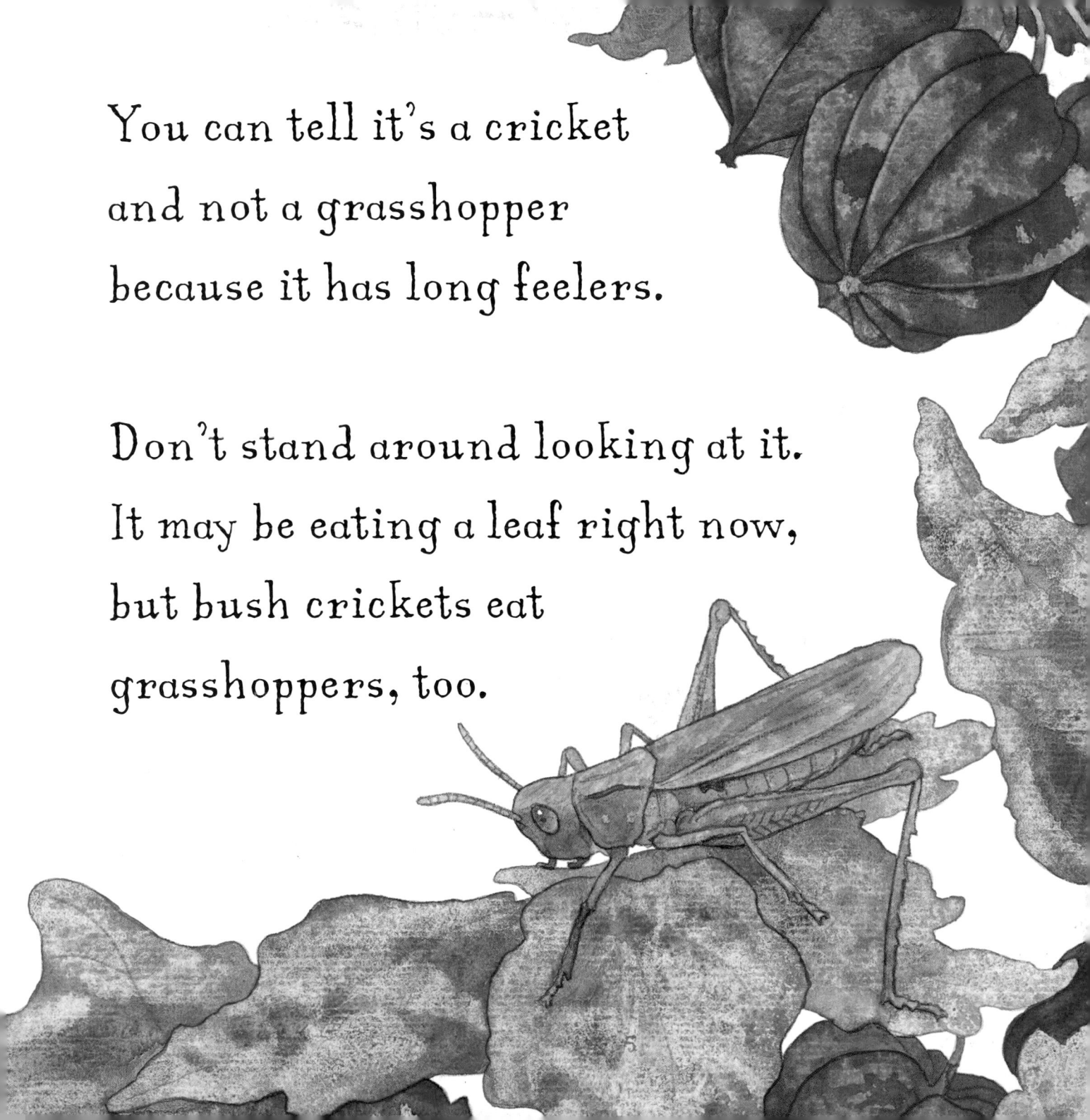

You can tell it's a cricket
and not a grasshopper
because it has long feelers.

Don't stand around looking at it.
It may be eating a leaf right now,
but bush crickets eat
grasshoppers, too.

Don't get caught
in a spiderweb.
Spiders eat grasshoppers.

Don't get too close
to a frog or a toad.
Frogs and toads
eat grasshoppers.

Watch out for birds.

Some birds eat
grasshoppers too.

It's a dangerous
world out there
in the grass.

Always be ready
to escape from danger.

You could fly–
except you're
not very good at flying.

You could hide.

You're very difficult
to see if you creep
down among
the grass stems.

Or you could hop.
After all, you ARE
a grasshopper.

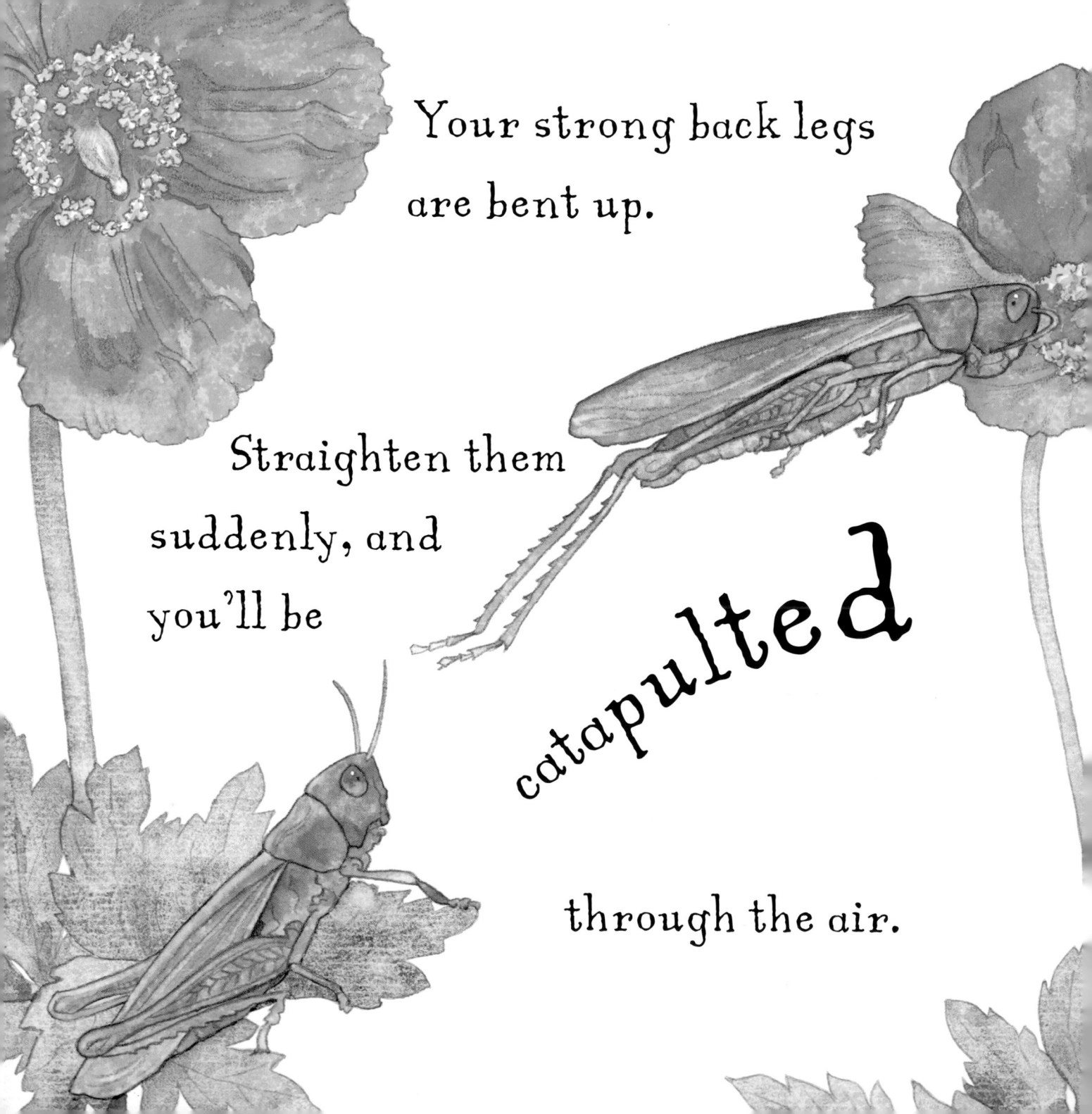

Your strong back legs
are bent up.

Straighten them
suddenly, and
you'll be

catapulted

through the air.

You can jump amazingly
high and travel an
amazingly long way.

You're very light,
and your skin is like a
suit of armor. You won't
hurt yourself when you land.

You have a row of tiny pegs on the inside of each leg. Pedal your legs up and down fast. The pegs rub against your wings and make a ticking, chirping noise.

Keep going for about twenty seconds.

Have a break.

Then start again.

If you are a male
grasshopper, chirp
loudly to attract a mate.

If you are a female
grasshopper, you can
chirp back if you want to.

The important thing
is to mate and lay eggs
for next year.

However, if your mother and father
look like this

or this

or this

you are not a grasshopper.

You are...

...a human child.

You don't have wings.

You don't have feelers.

You don't have ears in
the sides of your body.

You probably
can't jump
amazingly high.

Don't worry, you can do many things a grasshopper can't do.

Best of all, you can make music
without pedaling your legs
up and down.

Did You Know...

...the grasshoppers in this book are common green grasshoppers, but there are more than 7,000 different kinds of grasshoppers. Also, they are closely related to crickets, stick insects, cockroaches, and earwigs.

...a grasshopper can jump 20 times the length of its own body.

...the locust is a large, tropical grasshopper that is very good at flying. A swarm of locusts can eat a whole field of crops in one night.

...most grasshoppers die at the end of the summer, after they've laid their eggs.

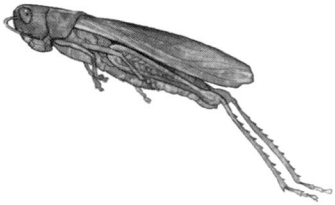